BEING AUTISTIC
(AND WHAT THAT ACTUALLY MEANS)

by the same author

Looking After Your Autistic Self
A Personalised Self-Care Approach to Managing
Your Sensory and Emotional Well-Being
Niamh Garvey
ISBN 978 1 83997 560 8
eISBN 978 1 83997 561 5

of related interest

Wired Differently – 30 Neurodivergent People You Should Know
Joe Wells
Illustrated by Tim Stringer
ISBN 978 1 78775 842 1
eISBN 978 1 78775 843 8

The Spectrum Girl's Survival Guide
How to Grow Up Awesome and Autistic
Siena Castellon
ISBN 978 1 78775 183 5
eISBN 978 1 78775 184 2

Can't Not Won't
A Story About A Child Who Couldn't Go To School
Eliza Fricker
ISBN 978 1 83997 520 2
eISBN 978 1 83997 521 9

The Awesome Autistic Guide to Being Proud
Feeling Good About Who You Are
Yenn Purkis and Tanya Masterman
ISBN 978 1 83997 736 7
eISBN 978 1 83997 737 4

BEING AUTISTIC

(And What That Actually Means)

Niamh Garvey

Illustrated by Rebecca Burgess

Jessica Kingsley Publishers
London and Philadelphia

First published in Great Britain in June 2024 by Jessica Kingsley Publishers
An imprint of John Murray Press

1

The fonts, layout and overall design of this book have been prepared
according to dyslexia-friendly principles. At JKP we aim to make our books'
content accessible to as many readers as possible.

A CIP catalogue record for this title is available from the British Library
and the Library of Congress

ISBN 978 1 80501 171 2
eISBN 978 1 80501 172 9

Printed and bound in Great Britain by Clays Ltd

Jessica Kingsley Publishers' policy is to use papers that are natural,
renewable and recyclable products and made from wood grown in
sustainable forests. The logging and manufacturing processes are expected
to conform to the environmental regulations of the country of origin.

Jessica Kingsley Publishers
Carmelite House
50 Victoria Embankment
London EC4Y 0DZ

www.jkp.com

John Murray Press
Part of Hodder & Stoughton Ltd
An Hachette Company

This book is dedicated to my three children:
Clara, Amelie and Iris. I love you all, and treasure how
each of you is unique in your own way. Niamh

To Lindsey: my journey into children's books started
with you, and I'm forever grateful for your passion and
talent that has carried me this far! Bex (Rebecca)

Acknowledgements

A brilliant bunch of people helped me to write this book, and I am so grateful to you all.

Thank you to my wonderful and vital proofreaders Cathal, Clara, Amelie, Laoi, Alanna, Brendan, Roisin, Nina, Charles, Theresa and Niamh Lucey. To my writer friends Eve, Aisling, Fran, Ciara, Olivia and Kevin, for their amazing ideas, and for pointing out the obvious, when I couldn't see it.

To Lisa Clarke at Jessica Kingsley Publishers, for believing in this book. To Abbie Howard and Matt Young from Jessica Kingsley Publishers, for all you do for me and for my books. To Micaela Connolly and Trish Barrett for lending your professional opinions. To the lecturers of University College Cork's Autism Diploma who taught me so much about how autism is so different for different people.

To my husband Cathal, and daughters Clara, Amelie and Iris, for making sure I had the time to write. Thank you, Trish, Nasser, Anne, Gavin, Rachel and Eoghan for ongoing support for my writing. Thank you, Rebecca Burgess, for bringing my words to life with your beautiful illustrations.

And lastly, thank you to all the autistic people who have shared their experiences and thoughts with me, without which I could not have done this book justice.

What is in this book and what page is it on?

PART 1
Welcome to being autistic!

Finding out you are autistic

Discovering that you are autistic just means that you have learned one more thing about yourself. You already knew lots of things about yourself, like what colour your eyes are, and what your favourite hobbies are, and what you like to eat... And now you know one more thing about yourself – you know that you are autistic.

You might be feeling confused about what it means to be autistic...

The answer to all of these is **no!**

You are still the same person that you always have been!

Did you know that you have been autistic since you were born?

Now that you know you are autistic, remember:

- You won't change into someone new.
- You don't have to change anything about yourself.
- You are still the same person that you always were.

What is neurodiversity?

In the past, people thought that all brains had to work the same way. They thought that everyone had to think the same way, learn the same way, and do things the same way.

Can you imagine if everyone thought exactly the same way?

People used to think that there was something wrong with people who learned differently, or people who wrote with their left hand instead of their right hand!

Thankfully, people eventually realised that trying to make everyone the same was not good for humans.

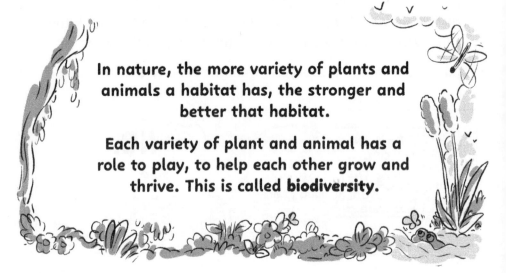

In nature, the more variety of plants and animals a habitat has, the stronger and better that habitat.

Each variety of plant and animal has a role to play, to help each other grow and thrive. This is called biodiversity.

Humans also do better when we have a variety of types of brains.

The natural variety in human brains is known as **neurodiversity**.

NEURODIVERSITY

NEURO = BRAINS
Diversity = Variety

The world is made up of many types of people, all of whom have different types of brains...

No no no, not like that*!!!* Our brain looks the same as everyone else's. It just thinks in different ways.

People who have a brain that thinks or works differently to a typical brain are called "neurodivergent".

Out of every ten people in the world, one or two are neurodivergent [1]. We all have many things that make up our **identity** (which basically means who we are).

Being neurodivergent is just one of those things.

When non-neurodivergent and neurodivergent people allow each other to grow and thrive in their own ways, humanity becomes stronger and better. Just like plants and animals in nature.

Autistic people are one type of neurodivergent people. There are many other types of neurodivergent people in the world, such as dyslexic, ADHD and dyspraxic people (you can read more about this in Part 3).

What does it mean to be autistic?

This is a hard question to answer because **no two autistic people are the same.**

Wait a minute...no two **non-autistic** people are the same either!

After all, the world is not made up of clones! That would just be weird...

Like all people, autistic people are all different to each other.

But! There are some things that are more common in autistic people. These are called **autistic traits**. Nearly everyone in the world has some autistic traits, but autistic people have **lots** of autistic traits, or their autistic traits are a **big** part of their daily life. **This is what makes us autistic!**

All autistic people have different autistic traits, and we are all completely different to each other. Long ago, people used to think that nearly all autistic people had the same autistic traits, but we now know that this is not true.

All autistic people have different lives, different traits, different interests, different skills and different hobbies.

Let's have a look at some of the most common autistic traits, so you can see which autistic traits you have, and which ones you do not have.

PART 2
Autistic traits

Predictability

We need a predictable plan!

Some (but not all) autistic people really want to know the plan for each day, and for everything they do. This makes life feel predictable.

Why do we need to know the plan? The world feels safer when we know the **who**, **what**, **where**, **when**, **why**, and **how long it lasts** of each plan. It also helps us when we know when we will get our **daily free time**.

Every day we like to:

- Know who we will see today.

- Know **what** will happen.

- Know **where** we will go.

- Know **when** things will happen and **how long it will last**.

- Know **why** the plan is happening.

- Know when we will get our **daily free time** to spend time on our **special interests**, or **relaxing**.

Stressed by surprises

Some autistic people find surprises really hard and stressful, because they were not part of the plan. Even good surprises can make us feel **all wrong**.

Change is challenging!

Some (but not all) autistic people find it hard when things change.

Some changes we can find hard are:

- Changes to the plan, or the order of the plan.

- Things at home, like where the furniture is, or who is at home after school.
- Things at school, like what chair we sit on or what subject we do on different days.
- People, like who our teacher is, who works in the local shop or who is at home at bedtime.
- Big changes, like moving house or changing school.
- Small changes, like the kitchen being painted a different colour or the bus driver taking a different route to the usual one.

When things change, it can make us feel odd or scared or like our bellies are full of butterflies.

Sometimes we want things to stay the same, even when we know that good things can happen with change. Even changes that we know are amazing can feel scary.

Unfortunately, things do change, and so do plans. That's just part of life, but it can be really frustrating for autistic people.

But fear not! We **can** get used to change. It just helps if we get a bit of time, and a warning, before change happens. This helps us to plan how to cope with the change.

Sensory experiences

The eight senses

Autistic people often have different sensory experiences to non-autistic people. This is because our senses work differently!

Our bodies are full of senses! They collect information about what is happening **inside** our bodies as well as **outside** our bodies.

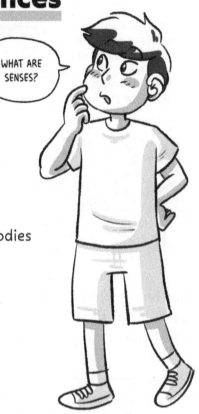

These are the eight main senses:

1 We see things using our sense of **sight**. Sometimes we love what we see. Sometimes we hate what we see.

2 We hear things using our sense of **sound**. Some sounds feel nice to us and some sounds feel awful.

3 Our sense of **taste** lets us know if we like something, or if we do not like it.

4 Our sense of **touch** tells us whether we like what we feel, or hate what we feel. It also tells us if what we touch hurts...

5 Our sense of **smell** tells us if we think a smell is lovely, or stinky.

6 Our sense of **balance** (some people call this the "vestibular sense") tells us about our balance and the position of our head. This helps us know if we are standing up straight, or are upside down, or about to fall over.

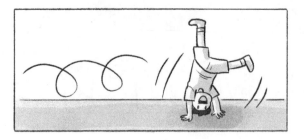

7 Our sense of our **body awareness** (some people call this the "proprioception sense") tells us about how close we are to other things, and tells us where we are in space.

No no no, not that kind of space... I mean the space around you.

Like the distance between you and the door.

And where your body parts are without you having to look at them...which is really helpful for making sure that you don't poke yourself in the eye with popcorn when you are watching a film. When our body awareness sense is not working so well, we are much more likely to poke ourselves in the eye with popcorn!

8 Our **internal** senses (some people call these the "interoception sense") tell us what is going on **inside** our body.

They tell us if we are hungry, thirsty, need to use the toilet, if we are hot or cold, if we feel pain, or if we need to fart.

They **also** tell us about the emotions we feel – whether we feel happy, sad, angry, disappointed, frustrated etc.

Sometimes autistic people find it really hard to know what their internal senses are trying to tell them. We might know we feel **something**, but not know what that something is!

Autistic senses

Autistic people's senses can work differently to non-autistic people. This means we collect information about what's going on inside our bodies, and in the world around, differently. This is why we can react differently to sensory things.

No two autistic people are the same, and we all **like** different sensory things to each other. We also all **dislike** different sensory things to each other.

How we react to sensory stuff doesn't always stay the same. Something we love one day we might hate the next day!

Sensory things that some (but not all) autistic people love love love

When we seek out a sensory experience that we love, we call it "sensory seeking".

Some things some autistic people love include:

Bouncing

Crunchy or chewy food

Being squished somewhere cosy

playing with water

Sensory things that some (but not all) autistic people hate hate hate

When we avoid a sensory experience that we dislike, we call it "sensory avoidance".

Some things some autistic people might hate include:

LOUD NOISES

Certain clothes

Some fabrics, tickling tags, scratchy seams on clothes

Certain sounds, even if other people don't notice them

Strong smells

crowds

TAG!

Being touched, especially by non-family members

some types of lights

Tilting backwards

Don't push too high!

certain food textures or tastes

Other people and our sensory differences

Sometimes it can really bother people when we **do** things because of our sensory differences.

And sometimes it can really bother people when we **don't** do things because of our sensory differences. They might even think we are just refusing to do something, when actually it's just really really hard for us to do it.

Stimming

Another sensory thing that some autistic people do is called **stimming**.

Stimming means doing something with your body again and again because it feels good. Most people stim a bit with their body, but some (though not all) autistic people stim **a lot!** Sometimes we stim because it feels good, and sometimes we do it to deal with stress.

There are hundreds of different ways that autistic people can stim:

- By repeating sounds or noises.

- By repeatedly moving their body a certain way, like spinning, or flapping their hands, or shaking their foot.

- By fidgeting with things, like pens, fidget toys, jewellery, or whatever they can find to fidget with!

- By thinking in repetitive ways, like counting numbers or thinking of poems, songs, words or prayers over and over again.

Communication confusion

Non-autistic people communicate differently to us!

There are lots and lots of reasons that autistic people can find communication hard.

WHAT EXACTLY IS COMMUNICATION? IS IT JUST TALKING?

No! Communication means sharing information with another person.

There are lots and lots of ways that people communicate, and talking is just one of them. Other ways we communicate include how we move our body, how we use our facial expressions, and how we use our voice or make noises.

Some people (both autistic and non-autistic) only communicate without speaking. They might communicate by writing or drawing, or using sign language or technology.

Everyone can find it hard to communicate with other people sometimes. Non-autistic people can sometimes find it hard to communicate with non-autistic people, and autistic people can find it hard to communicate with other autistic people. It's normal!

But! It can be **extra** hard for autistic and non-autistic people to communicate well together. This is neither person's fault; we are just more likely to communicate and think differently to each other.

When two people whose brains work differently communicate with each other, both of them can misunderstand what the other person is trying to say.

A well-known autistic man called Damien Milton calls this the "double empathy problem". When people experience the world differently (like autistic and non-autistic people do), they can find it hard to understand each other. Neither person communicates incorrectly; they just communicate differently to each other [2].

This can cause a lot of confusion!

For example, a non-autistic person might have learned that giving someone a hug shows the person that they are happy to be with them.

But an autistic person might not like hugs, and might feel unsafe in a hug. We might need to explain our differences to other people, so that we can find a way to understand each other. This helps us communicate with each other.

Sometimes we can find it hard to know what other people are trying to tell us.

And sometimes other people find it hard to understand what we are trying to tell them.

Some (but not all) autistic people make sense of what people are saying at a different speed to other people. This is called our "processing speed". Sometimes it might take us a bit (or a lot) longer to process what someone is saying to us, and how to react.

Conversations can be confusing!

Having a conversation with another person is not only talking. It also includes listening to each other, and sharing ideas or information with each other.

There are lots and lots of reasons that autistic people can find conversations confusing.

Sometimes it can be really hard to know how to join in (or how to leave!) a conversation that other people are having.

Sometimes we find it hard to know when it is okay to talk, and when it is not okay to talk.

Sometimes it takes us a bit more time to think about and understand what people are saying, especially if they change the subject quickly.

Sometimes other people don't want to talk about the same things as we do, and we want to talk about them all day long!

Sometimes we can feel left out of a conversation that we want to be a part of.

Sometimes we can find it easier to have a conversation with just one other person, as group conversations can be hard to keep up with. It's hard when lots of different people are talking at the same time!

Conversation clues

When we communicate with other people, they tell us things with their face, their eyes, their body, the tone of their voice, and more. These are all called **conversation clues**.

A conversation clue is supposed to tell you something about what the other person is saying.

It would be nice to think that when someone is talking to us we simply have to listen to their words to understand what they are telling us.

Unfortunately, when we have a conversation with someone, we are supposed to pay attention to more than just their words.

Believe me, I know. But it's true! A lot of autistic people find it hard to recognise and understand conversation clues.

There are four main conversation clues.

TONE OF VOICE

Tone of voice is the musical sound of the voice. It gives us clues about what the other person is feeling, which is supposed to help us to understand what they are saying. We often find it hard to understand what someone's tone of voice is supposed to be telling us.

There are lots of ways that people use their tone of voice to communicate more than their words alone.

When people speak, they might change how loudly or quietly they speak. This can give us a clue about how they are feeling.

Their voice might get quiet and whispery if they are scared.

Sometimes people change the musical sound, or melody, of words in the sentence, almost like it's a song.

It might get extra musical if they are feeling amazed.

Sometimes people make some words in their sentence sound louder than others, which means that the loud word is really important.

Something that can be really confusing for autistic people is that the same tone of voice clues can mean totally different things!

People's voices might get loud and shouty if they feel angry or shocked.

Or they might get loud and shouty when they are excited or really happy.

Sometimes autistic people have unusual tones of voice. We might speak without changing the tone of our voice, or we might use a different tone of voice to what people expect, when we want to explain our feelings.

Sometimes people can find the sound of our autistic voices confusing, especially if we speak with a different accent to our family and friends.

As you can see, tone of voice clues are confusing.

We often have to ask other people to explain their tone of voice, to make sure that we understand what they want us to.

BODY LANGUAGE

When people want to tell us something, they do not always use spoken words. Sometimes they tell us things by moving certain parts of their body. This is called "body language". Some (but not all) autistic people can find body language a bit or **very** confusing.

Sometimes people use body language to tell us something without using spoken words.

Sometimes people use body language to tell us more information than their words.

Sometimes people's body language helps other people know how they feel.

Sometimes we use our body language to help us explain what we want.

Some autistic people find it really hard to recognise or understand body language. This can make it hard for us to fully understand what someone is trying to communicate to us.

FACIAL EXPRESSIONS

People often change their facial expressions to tell other people about how they feel or what they are thinking.

Some (but not all) autistic people can find it hard to understand what someone's facial expression means.

Sometimes we find it hard to use facial expressions ourselves, or use them in different ways to other people. When people we are talking to do not understand this, it can be really confusing for them.

Sometimes non-autistic people think that we are trying to tell them something through our facial expressions, even though we are not. We might not be thinking about our facial expressions at all!

Some people even use emoji facial expressions when they are communicating by text, or online, to give us a clue about what they are saying or how they feel.

EYE CONTACT

Eye contact means looking another person in the eye. A lot of people like to look each other in the eye when they are having a conversation.

People make eye contact with us to:

- Show us that they are talking to us.
- Show us that they want to talk to us.
- Show us that they are listening to us.
- Feel a connection with us.
- Look for clues about how we feel.

Some (but not all) autistic people do not like eye contact. Lots of autistic people use little tricks to avoid eye contact, like looking at someone's nose instead of at their eyes!

Sometimes eye contact can feel fine to us, sometimes it can feel horrible, and sometimes it can even feel sore.

Everyone uses different amounts of eye contact. Some people use a little, and some people (both autistic and non-autistic) use a **lot** of eye contact (and it can feel like too much eye contact, even for non-autistic people!).

STOP LOOKING IN MY EYES. IT FEELS LIKE YOU'RE BURNING THEM!

Sometimes people use their eyes to tell you how they feel, **like if they are surprised, angry or sad.**

Non-autistic people don't always know that autistic people can find eye contact hard, and might feel upset when we do not look them in the eye.

When we do not look people in the eye, they might worry that:

- We are not listening to them.
- We are bored by what they are saying.
- We are not being friendly.
- We are being dishonest or lying.
- We feel afraid.
- We feel ashamed.
- We are hiding our feelings.

But don't worry!! Autistic people do **not** have to force themselves to make eye contact.

Other people should not ask us to make eye contact when they know it does not feel safe, or okay, for us.

We can just explain that we are listening, that we are interested, but we simply do not feel okay when we make eye contact. Or we can make listening noises every now and then (but not non-stop!), like "mm-hm", or say things like "yeah" or "okay", to show people that we are listening.

Silly sayings

Something that some (but not all) autistic people get confused by is "sayings". This is not surprising, since "sayings" usually make no sense!

One type of "saying" is called an "idiom". These are sentences that mean something different to what the words in the sentence actually mean.

For example, the saying "caught red handed" does not mean that someone has been caught with red hands; it actually means that they have been found doing something that they are not allowed to do.

Most sayings did actually make sense at some point in history, which is how they became a saying in the first place. They are confusing because they no longer make sense nowadays.

Answer: There was once a law (a long, long time ago) that said

61

someone could only be found guilty of killing a pig if they were found with the pig's blood on their hands. If they were found with pig's blood on their hands, that is, with red hands, this meant that they were guilty and would be punished. If they had killed the pig but had clean hands, they could not be found guilty and punished for the crime.

OOHHH

CAN YOU EXPLAIN THE SAYING "PUT A SOCK IN IT"? PEOPLE ARE ALWAYS SAYING THAT TO ME.

Answer: Before telephones, TVs and car radios, people used machines called gramophones to play music. The music came out of a big horn, and there was no volume control. When people wanted the music to be quieter, they would push socks into the horn, to quieten the sound coming out. This is why people say "put a sock in it" when they want someone to hush and quieten down.

Answer: It is thought that this saying began in England (a long, long time ago), before city streets had drainage systems to collect rainwater. When it rained heavily, the roads would flood, and carry stray cats and dogs along in the floods. It therefore looked as if it had rained cats and dogs.

Jokes

Some (but not all) autistic people find it hard to understand jokes.

Some (but not all) autistic people often have to think really **really really** hard about why a joke is funny. It might take us longer than other people to understand a joke, which can be a bit embarrassing if you suddenly get the joke later than everyone else!

Sometimes we don't even realise that someone is joking, and sometimes people might think we are joking when we are not!

Some (but not all) autistic people find it hard to know when it is okay to make a joke, and when it is not okay to make the same joke.

Sarcasm

One really confusing type of humour is called sarcasm. Sarcasm is a type of joke where someone says something but they mean the opposite of what they say. People usually give clues that they are being sarcastic, but it is not always easy for autistic people to spot those clues.

Here are some clues for when someone is being sarcastic:

1 The person exaggerates one word and makes that word sound really long, as if they are stretching the word.

2 The person might use body language or facial expressions to show that they mean something different to their words. They might roll their eyes or put their hands on their hips.

3 Another type of sarcasm is called deadpan sarcasm. This is when the person says something in a low monotone tone of voice (a dull, boring voice, with no sing-song changes in the sound of the voice), but they mean the opposite of what they are saying.

Trouble with talking

Some (but not all) autistic people have a little bit or a **lot** of trouble with talking. This might be all the time, or it might only happen sometimes, like when we feel really nervous, scared or excited.

Some autistic people find it hard to **stop** talking, especially when they are talking about their special interests!

Some autistic people can only speak a few words, or might say the same sentences over and over again. This is called "echolalia", because we make an echo out of our words.

68

Some autistic people cannot speak any words at all, or can only say a few words. Even if someone cannot speak, they **do understand and hear** everything that everyone else is saying.

Just because someone cannot speak doesn't mean they have nothing to say! They can still join in the conversation, even if they cannot speak. There are lots of ways to do this without speaking.

They might point at pictures.

They might use sign language, and talk with their hands.

AND THEN SHE SLIPPED ON A BANANA SKIN!

Hahahahahaha!

Some autistic people who cannot speak, or who have difficulty talking, use technology to do the talking for them. This is called Augmented and Alternative Communication (also known as AAC).

By using AAC, we can tell the computer, tablet or phone app what we want to say by tapping symbols or pictures, or writing words, and then the technology turns the message into words spoken out loud.

Remember, many people use technology to do their talking, whether they can or cannot speak. This includes texting on a phone, sending a message on social media or chatting to someone by typing while playing computer games.

Saying something without speaking out loud can give us more time to think about what we want to say and how we want to say it. This is especially helpful when we are upset, or when we need to tell someone something that we find hard to talk about.

Special interests

Most autistic people have one or more really **really really** special interests.

A special interest is something we absolutely **love** to do, or something that we **love** to learn about. It might be our special interest for only a few days, a few weeks, a few months, a few years, or our whole life!

Having a special interest makes autistic people feel good. We might even forget to do other things because we are so**oOOO** happy and focused when we are engaged in our special interest.

Some autistic people have more than one special interest. Just think about what you love doing, or something you always want to learn about, or something that you think about **a lot.**

Perhaps you are...

An art addict   A devourer of books   A football fanatic

An animal adorer   A brilliant baker   A maths maniac
(or a bad baker, but you love it anyway...)

A history hunter   A dinosaur dictionary   A video-gamer

A wargaming wizard

A secret spy master

A locomotive lover

A fantasy fan

A musical master

Social stuff

Socialising

Socialising means spending time with other people. Sometimes we socialise for fun or friendships. Sometimes socialising is just a part of our day, like hanging out with other people at lunchtime in school.

Some (but not all) autistic people can find socialising hard. There are lots of reasons for this:

Some autistic people find it hard to make friends.

Some (but not all) autistic people find it hard to keep friends, especially when they do not have the same interests or hobbies.

Sometimes other people do not understand our autism, and might get annoyed if we do not behave the same way that they do. This can be because people find our autistic differences confusing, until they are explained to them.

Sometimes we can find it hard to join in socially because we are tired, or because of sensory stuff.

Predictable socialising

Some (but not all) autistic people only like socialising when everything feels organised, and goes according to plan.

Sometimes autistic people expect things to always be the same when they meet other people, and can feel all wrong when things change. This can make socialising really hard.

Sometimes autistic people can find it really hard to finish socialising, because they do not want the fun to end. We often find transitions hard. (A transition is stopping one activity and starting another, like stopping playing in order to go home.)

Masking

Some (but not all) autistic people try to hide their autistic traits when they are around other people. This is more common when we are around people who do not understand autism, if we are afraid people will judge us for doing things differently to them. Some people call this "camouflaging", and some people call it "masking".

Sometimes we can feel like we need to camouflage our autism, so that we do not stand out as any different.

Some autistic people mask in order to pretend that they understand the conversation, even when they are really confused! This is usually because we are afraid people might think there is something wrong with us if we don't follow the conversation and get all the jokes.

Sometimes autistic people don't even notice when they are masking.

There are some situations where we are expected to follow certain rules or behave in a certain way. This might mean we need to behave in ways that don't come naturally to us. This is a type of masking, but non-autistic people do this too, to show respect, or to allow more people access or to join in.

The problem with masking is that it takes a lot of effort, and can be exhausting.

If we are working hard to mask our autistic differences, it can cause our body to feel stressed. This feeling of stress can build up inside us until we feel really overwhelmed.

Remember! It's totally okay to be autistic, and it is totally okay to be different!

The more the people around us learn to understand and respect our autism, the easier it will be for us to just be ourselves.

Social exhaustion

Lots of autistic people **love** socialising. Just like non-autistic people, we love to have fun, we love to have friends, we love to feel included, and we love to know that we are important to other people.

But! Even when we enjoy socialising, we can still get really tired during it, or after it. A clue that we have had enough socialising is that we might start feeling cranky or overwhelmed or exhausted.

READY TO PLAY!

A LITTLE TIRED

FEELING OVERWHELMED

NO MORE ENERGY

Sometimes we might not notice that we are getting socially exhausted, but when we get home we might feel overwhelmed or extremely tired, upset or angry, or we might have a meltdown or a shutdown.

When you think about all the extra energy we have to spend when socialising, it's no wonder we get exhausted! It takes extra energy to:

- Look for conversation clues.
- Figure out conversation clues.
- Think about whether we understand what someone is saying.
- Figure out when people are joking or being serious.
- Deal with the **big** emotions we might be feeling when around other people.

- Cope with sensory stuff.
- Figure out the correct response.
- Figure out when to talk without interrupting.

Sometimes we get so tired of being with other people that we feel like we just need a break alone.

Social games

Some (but not all) autistic people can find playing games with other people really fun, or it can be really hard.

The same game might be fun one day and really hard another day, especially if...

- The rules change.

- We don't win the game.

- The rules don't seem fair.

- We have to stop playing before the game is finished.

- When we do not agree on the rules with the other people playing.

Feelings

Not knowing what you are feeling

Some (but not all) autistic people find it hard to understand, or recognise, the feelings in their bodies. The proper word for this is "alexithymia".

Our body gives us clues about what we need by making us feel things in our body. For example, we feel thirsty when we need a drink, or tired when we need sleep. We also feel clues when we are experiencing an emotion, such as happiness or sadness.

Some of us don't feel these clues, or sometimes we do feel them but do not know what they mean.

Sometimes we know we feel all wrong, but we do not know **why** we feel all wrong.

Sometimes we might know that we feel **something** in our body, but we do not know if it is an emotion, or if it is a clue that our body needs something.

Sometimes we do not notice when we start to feel emotions, like sadness or anger. We might only notice we feel the emotion when the feeling becomes so strong that it feels **absolutely enormous!**

Enormous emotions

For some (but not all) autistic people, the feelings that tell us we are experiencing an emotion can feel absolutely **enormous!**

Our emotions can feel so strong that it can feel as if they are taking over our whole body.

Even emotions that are supposed to feel good can make us feel all wrong because we feel them so strongly.

When our emotions become **too big**, we can feel overwhelmed. When we are overwhelmed, we might not be able to do the normal things we usually do, like sleep, eat, drink or communicate.

Empathy

Another thing that
autistic people can find
hard is dealing with
other people's feelings and
emotions.

Some (but not all) autistic people
can feel empathy differently to
non-autistic people.

When we recognise that someone else
has an uncomfortable feeling, like
sadness, fear or pain, we might feel
sympathy, or empathy.

When we feel **sympathy**, it means that we
recognise that another person feels an
uncomfortable feeling, and we feel pity for
them. While sympathy is fine, we are not actually connecting
with the other person and how they feel. It therefore does
not really help the other person to feel better.

When we feel **empathy**, we recognise what someone is feeling, and we **imagine** how they are feeling and feel it with them. This connection can help the other person feel better – almost as though we are sharing the burden of their difficult emotion.

To show someone that we feel empathy for them, it is nice to show them that we care and want to support them. We can do this by being there for them, almost as if we are sharing their feelings, so that they don't have to feel it so much on their own.

Sometimes, we feel too much empathy, and it can feel like whenever someone else feels an emotion, we feel it too, which can be overwhelming – like if we see someone else crying, it might make us feel like crying too!

When some autistic people feel empathy towards someone, they can find it hard to know what to say or do to show the other person that they understand and care about how they feel. We might not know what facial expression to use. Sometimes this can make people think that we do not feel empathy, but actually we just do not know how to **show** our empathy.

Some autistic people find it really hard to recognise what another person is feeling, especially if they find it hard to read their facial expressions, body language or understand sarcasm.

When we do not recognise that someone wants us to show them empathy, it can look like we do not feel empathy towards them. But that's not true; autistic people do feel empathy!

But! We do not always recognise the conversation clues (especially body language and facial expressions) that are supposed to tell us how other people are feeling. Therefore, it is really helpful when people tell us clearly how they are feeling. This gives us the opportunity to feel and show our empathy.

Anxiety

Anxiety is a normal
feeling that most people
experience sometimes,
or many times, in their
lives. It is supposed to
be a helpful feeling – to tell
us when we are in danger, or to
remind us not to forget something,
or to help us to keep ourselves safe.

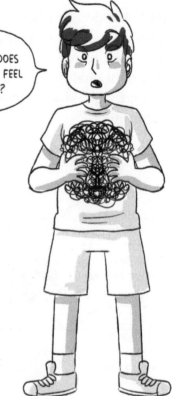

WHAT DOES ANXIETY FEEL LIKE?

Sometimes we can feel anxious
even when we are safe, when there
is no danger, and when we have
nothing serious to worry about.
Some (but not all) autistic people
feel this type of anxiety more often
than non-autistic people.

Anxiety feels different for everyone.
When we feel anxious, we might
experience the emotion of worry or
nervousness.

We might also feel wrong in our bodies. We might get a
headache, a dry mouth, nausea, a twisty-turny feeling
inside our tummies, or need to go to the toilet more often.
We might also clench our muscles, clench our jaw, cry or
start shaking. When we feel really anxious, it can feel as
though it is hard to breathe, even though we are actually
able to breathe well. Sometime people do repetitive actions
when they are anxious, like jittering their legs, or chewing
the cuffs of their jumper.

Sometimes we feel anxious for a reason:

Like when the plan changes.

Or when we do not know what to expect.

Or when our sensory system is overwhelmed.

Sometimes we feel anxious about going somewhere, or doing something, even though we want to do it. This can be confusing!

Sometimes we feel anxious and have no idea why!

All emotions go away again, even anxiety. Sometimes we can feel like an emotion is so big that it will last forever. Even when anxiety feels **enormous**, remember that it will go away again.

What can help anxiety go away?

- Doing exercise.
- Doing something to do with a special interest (but not **too** much of it...our special interests can't be the only thing we do!).
- Eating a healthy meal.
- Taking a drink.
- Sleeping or resting.
- Telling a person who we feel safe with about our anxiety.
- Having a shower or a bath.
- Doing a beloved sensory activity.
- Going out into nature for fresh air.
- Spending time with people we love.

Meltdowns

When some (but not all) autistic people get totally overwhelmed by their emotions, sometimes they can have a meltdown.

A MELTDOWN? AM I GOING TO ACTUALLY MELT?

No, no, no. Nobody actually melts in a meltdown. It's more like an explosion.

I'M GOING TO EXPLODE?! AAAAHHHH!!

No no no, we don't actually explode in a meltdown. It just **feels** like our emotions explode.

Meltdowns are different for all autistic people. They can make us feel like we have lost control of our body, our emotions and even our brain!

Meltdowns only last for a short amount of time, and usually happen when something totally stresses us out. They are more likely to happen when we are exhausted, hungry or thirsty, or when we have had too much sensory stress and feel like we cannot cope any more.

Remember! Autistic people do not always recognise when they are hungry or thirsty or tired. So when we feel close to a meltdown, it is a good idea to ask ourselves when we last ate and drank, in case we are hungry or thirsty without knowing it.

Meltdowns can feel horrible and we might do things that we normally would never do. This is not our fault; it happens because we have lost control of ourselves for a little while.

After a meltdown, we might feel really exhausted, like all the energy has drained out of us.

The good news is that when we start paying attention, we are often able to start noticing what things make us more likely to have a meltdown. This can help us to have fewer meltdowns, or wait to have the meltdown somewhere we feel safe.

When we feel a meltdown coming, we can try to think about what might help the meltdown go away, like taking a break with a snack, a drink and one of our special interests.

Knowing what causes us to have a meltdown can help us to take a break, ask for help or use something to help us cope with sensory stuff before we reach meltdown.

Remember! Meltdowns never last forever!! They can feel as though they last a long time, but all meltdowns do end.

Shutdowns

A shutdown feels like our mind takes a little break from working properly. It can happen when we are overwhelmed, when we feel like we can't cope with our emotions and just need to switch off and recharge.

It's not unlike a computer shutting down...

Some autistic people go somewhere to hide when they need a shutdown, like a cosy nook, or into bed, or behind a chair. We might cover our ears or close our eyes to block out any sensory stuff that is annoying us.

Sometimes shutdowns happen suddenly when we get suddenly stressed or overwhelmed. We usually get a clue that a shutdown is about to happen, such as a peculiar feeling in our body that tells us we need to reset and recharge.

In a shutdown, some (but not all) autistic people might stop talking, listening or moving around.

Like meltdowns, shutdowns don't last forever. Having a rest, a sleep, watching our favourite TV show, listening to our favourite audiobooks or doing one of our special interests can help us get through a shutdown. Food and drinks help too! Mostly, we need to be patient and kind to ourselves, and know we will be able to restart again soon.

Learning styles

Different learning styles

Some (but not all) autistic people learn in different ways to non-autistic people. This doesn't mean that all autistic people learn the same way as each other. It just means that we often need things taught to us in a slightly different way, or in a different type of environment to non-autistic people.

Remember!! No two autistic people are the same, so it is really important that we figure out what helps each of us to learn.

Some autistic people learn better when they can see and hold things, rather than just a teacher telling them about what they want them to learn. It can be much easier for us to understand a question or a calculation when we can see real things, rather than being asked to imagine things.

Some autistic people learn better when they are alone, in a very quiet room. It can be hard to think in a really busy classroom with lots of noise!

Some autistic people learn better in smaller groups.
But some find it easier to work by themselves, rather than
in a group.

Some (but not all) autistic people focus better when there is nice sensory stuff going on, like having music on, or chewing gum, or sitting on a wobbly cushion or gym ball.

Some autistic people can think better when they are moving. We often need to move a lot throughout the day, and might need to take breaks from our lessons to move.

When we walk or swing or bounce, it can help us to remember what we have learned, and can help us to figure things out.

Some autistic people find it hard to learn or remember how to do something unless they do it themselves.

Some autistic children learn better in smaller classes with fewer students, but some learn best in big classes with lots of students. Some autistic children do some activities or subjects in small classes, and do other activities and subjects in big classes.

Some of us really need to know what to expect, and we learn better when we know what we will be learning about today, and what subjects come first, and when we will have a break.

"Fierce focus" versus "flighty focus"

Some (but not all) autistic people can focus **really really** deeply, for a **really really** long time on one thing that interests them **(fierce focus)**.

But! We can find it really hard to focus on things that don't interest us **(flighty focus)**.

Some people say that this is because autistic people have "monotropic minds" [3]. A monotropic mind has a really big interest in a small amount of things, whereas a polytropic mind tends to have a smaller amount of interest, but in a lot more things.

We can find it hard when we are told to change the subject, as our monotropic minds want to stay focused on what interests us.

118

Our focus can affect how we cope with **transitions**. A transition is when we change from one activity to another, or from one place to another. Knowing a change is coming helps us to feel calm when that change happens.

Having extra time to prepare for the change helps us feel ready to **stop** what we are focused on and ready to **start** the next activity.

In school, it can be hard for autistic people when one activity or subject ends and a new one begins. When we are focused on something, it can feel wrong when we have to stop before we feel ready.

When autistic people are really focused on one thing, it can be hard for us to notice what is happening around us.

Our monotropic minds can be amazing, and mean that we can notice details that other people miss, or learn huge amounts of information about things that interest us.

Organisation frustration

Getting organised is hard!

Most autistic people feel better when things feel organised. Being organised helps things feel predictable, which helps us to feel calm and in control.

BUT!! Some (but not all) autistic people find it really hard to get themselves organised. This can be really frustrating.

This is because the "organisation station" in our brains works differently! The proper term for the brain's "organisation station" is "executive function". This controls the part of our brain that is in charge of getting things done.

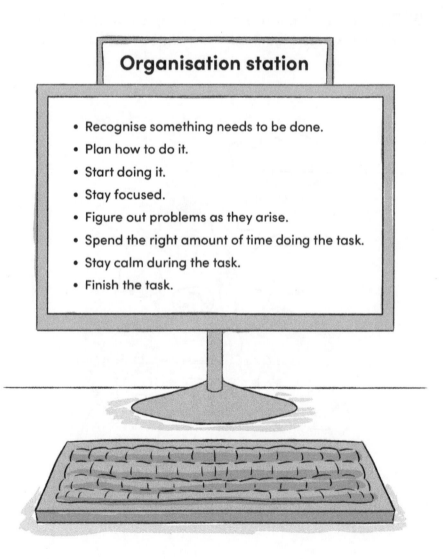

Organisation station

- Recognise something needs to be done.
- Plan how to do it.
- Start doing it.
- Stay focused.
- Figure out problems as they arise.
- Spend the right amount of time doing the task.
- Stay calm during the task.
- Finish the task.

Some autistic people spend a lot of time and energy making sure that they stay organised, so that they can try to keep things feeling predictable.

Some autistic people love it when things are well organised, but find it really hard to stay organised, especially if their monotropic mind is fiercely focused on one thing, and therefore forgets everything else they are supposed to do!

Sometimes autistic people can stay organised when they feel calm. But when we get stressed or overwhelmed, our "organisation station" stops working.

Creativity

Thinking outside the box

When people talk about autistic people, they often say that they "think outside the box". This is because we are good at looking at things in a different way to how other people look at things.

We often have creative minds, and we can be great at thinking up new ways to do things.

We are often brilliant at solving problems. It can be hard to solve problems when we do not feel calm, but we can come up with **amazing** solutions to problems when we are calm and content.

Many autistic people create beautiful things, like music, books and art. Because we think differently, we often come up with new ideas, and have wonderful imaginations. Some people say we are "original thinkers" because of this!

Creative happiness

Some autistic people feel happiest when they are creating, especially when they use their creative minds and their special interests together.

Body movement

Our active bodies move more!

Some (but not all) autistic people move their bodies a bit or **very** differently to non-autistic people.

TAPPING MY FINGERS TOGETHER HELPS ME THINK.

Some autistic people feel the need to move their body nearly all the time.

We might do lots of different movements, or we might move in the same way over and over again.

THIS IS THE **FIFTH TIME** I'VE STUBBED MY TOE TODAY! WHY ARE MY FEET NOT GOING WHERE I **WANT** THEM TODAY!

Some (but not all) autistic people can feel like their body forgets to listen to their brain, and doesn't always do what they tell it to do!

Some (but not all) autistic people like to walk on their tiptoes.

Moving our bodies in the same way again and again is a type of stimming. This can help us stay calm and focused. We might tap our fingers, fidget with our hands, spin around and around, rock our bodies or flap our hands.

PART 3

Other things some autistic people have

In this part

There are some differences, or difficulties, that are more common in autistic people or in the families of autistic people. Some autistic people have none of these other differences or difficulties, and some have more than one.

It is helpful to know if you have one or more of these differences or difficulties, so you can get the right help and support. Here are some examples.

Dyspraxia/developmental coordination disorder (DCD)

This is a difficulty with certain movements and coordination. Coordination means using more than one part of the body at a time, for example, using both arms at the same time.

For a dyspraxic person, when the brain tells the body to do a certain movement, the message gets scrambled up along the way, and the movement can be clumsy or wrong.

A lot of autistic people have some difficulty with coordination, but people with dyspraxia have a lot of difficulty.

People with dyspraxia can find it really hard to do everyday skills, like tying shoelaces, opening a food packet, playing sport, catching and throwing a ball, balance and riding a bike. They might accidentally injure themselves a lot, by falling, tripping over or walking into things. They might find it hard to follow directions, and know which is left and which is right. It can be very challenging for dyspraxic people when the environment changes, like if furniture moves or if they are told to sit at a different desk to the one they are used to.

Dyslexia

Dyslexic people have difficulty with reading, writing and spelling. Their brains make sense of what they see in a different way, and letters and words do not look the same to a dyslexic person as they do to a non-dyslexic person. Some people with dyslexia say that the letters move or dance when they are trying to read. Some dyslexic people can feel like their brain is tricking them, and turning the letters they read upside down, or back to front!

Dyslexic people can also have difficulty following instructions or orders that have more than one step. A dyslexic brain can find it hard to organise information step by step. Dyslexic people might also find it hard to learn things like the days of the week, or the months of the year, off by heart. Being dyslexic has nothing to do with being clever; it just means the brain scrambles up the reading messages. Some extremely clever people are dyslexic.

Some dyslexic people can read better when they read using coloured paper, coloured film over the words or glasses with coloured lenses.

Dyscalculia

This is a difficulty with certain maths skills, including learning the times tables, adding and subtracting. The part of the brain that works on adding and subtracting does not do its job properly. Besides difficulty with sums, dyscalculia can also cause difficulties with calculating money and telling the time.

Some people with dyscalculia are really good at hard maths problems, but need a calculator for simple sums.

ADHD

This is also called "attention deficit hyperactivity disorder". People with ADHD have difficulty staying focused on things they are not interested in, even when they know it is really important, and they really want to stay focused. They might be able to focus really well on things that they are really interested in. It is not their fault that they get distracted easily.

People with ADHD might also be very impulsive, which means they find it hard (or cannot) stop themselves from carrying out an idea that comes into their head.

Some people with ADHD have hyperactive bodies, and move non-stop, fidget all the time, and might like to run around a lot. Some have a hyperactive brain, and their thoughts jump from topic to topic really fast. This can make them speak really really fast, and interrupt other people a lot (because they feel like they have to say something quickly before they lose their thought!).

Hypermobility

This is also known as being double-jointed, which means extra-bendy joints. A joint is a part of the body where two bones meet, like at the elbow, shoulder or knee.

For some people this might just mean having more flexible joints.

For others, being hypermobile can make certain activities more tiring, like handwriting or walking. It can also make it easier to get injured, or might mean more pain in the body. People who are hypermobile need to do plenty of exercise to make sure their muscles are stronger, so they can support their bendy joints.

People (like the author of this book) who are extremely hypermobile and stretchy might have hypermobile Ehlers-Danlos syndrome (hEDS), which means they are extra extra bendy!

Learning difficulties

Some autistic people, just like some non-autistic people, have a learning difficulty that affects how they learn how to do everyday tasks. Children with a learning difficulty might need a lot of extra help with everyday things, like getting dressed, eating, learning school lessons, playing and communicating. Some children with a learning difficulty go to a special school, which has teachers and staff who know exactly how to help them to learn and gain new skills.

PART 4

Now you know what it means to be autistic... what's next?

Being autistic is just one part of us. There are still lots of other parts of us that have nothing to do with being autistic, like whether we like music, or whether we are good at a sport, or which are our favourite subjects to learn about.

Many autistic people have similar lives to most non-autistic people. We grow up, we get a job, we fall in love, we travel, we buy a house.

Just like non-autistic people, there are also some autistic people who do not do these things, and that is fine too.

I DON'T THINK I WANT TO GET MARRIED AND HAVE KIDS. I'D RATHER WORK IN A BOOKSHOP, READ LOTS OF BOOKS, AND SPEND TIME WITH MY FAMILY AND FRIENDS. THAT SOUNDS LIKE A GREAT LIFE TO ME.

And just like non-autistic people, we can use our own unique skills and interests to come up with our own unique goals and dreams. We all need to figure out what we are good at, what we need to work harder at, and what skills we need more help with.

There are lots of great things about being autistic. We can be very passionate, and often believe strongly in our values and morals. We can be excellent friends, and are often very funny! We can be brilliant workers, especially when we find a job to do with our special interests. We can have very creative ideas, and can develop all sorts of skills.

Just like non-autistic people, some autistic people in history have done amazing things. Many autistic people have changed the world for the better, by having:

Composed beautiful music.

Created wonderful art.

Solved big problems.

Come up with new and amazing ways to do things.

Written great books.

Been environmental activists.

But*!!* **Most** autistic people, like **most** non-autistic people, live fairly normal lives. We are not all geniuses, we are not all amazing at one big skill, and we are not all going to change the world in enormous ways. And that is okay too!

Sometimes being autistic can make certain parts of everyday life harder, especially when:

- The environment has sensory things we dislike.
- People around us don't understand or respect our autistic differences.
- Our emotions feel too big or out of control.

Thankfully, there are a lot of people who can help us feel more comfortable in the world. There are professionals who are specially trained to help make daily life easier. Lots of these professionals are autistic themselves! It can also be really helpful to get to know other autistic people, as we can all learn tips from each other.

Occupational therapists can help us understand our sensory differences, and teach us to look after our own sensory system. This can help us feel calmer, and we have fewer meltdowns or shutdowns.

Schools and teachers can make changes to our day – like giving us movement breaks, allowing us to use fidget toys, helping us to join in socially, and using visual timetables so the day is predictable.

Speech therapists can help improve our ability to join in socially and find a way to communicate with other people.

Play therapists or psychologists can help us to manage our emotions, especially anxiety.

Educational psychologists can try to figure out what would help us to learn, and what our schools can do to make sure we feel calm and safe in school.

It can really help us to find daily life easier when our family understands our autism. We could ask family and friends to read this book, so that they can understand us better. Explaining which parts of autism affect us, and what other people can do to help us, can make life much better for us.

Remember!! The most important person to support our autistic self is ourselves! The more we learn to understand our own autism, and what helps us to feel calm and content, the better life gets. Some days can feel really hard, and some days will feel brilliant and full of joy. That's just life. So make the most of it!

The End!

References

1. DCEG (Division of Cancer Epidemiology & Genetics), NIH (National Cancer Institute) (2022) "Neurodiversity." 25 April. https://dceg.cancer.gov/about/diversity-inclusion/inclusivity-minute/2022/neurodiversity

2. Milton, D.E.M. (2012) "On the ontological status of autism: The 'double empathy problem'." *Disability & Society* 27, 6, 883–887.

3. Murray, D., Lesser, M. and Lawson, W. (2005) "Attention, monotropism and the diagnostic criteria for autism." *Autism* 9, 2, 139–156.

Index

(Use this to find out what page something you want to know about is on.)

About the author

Niamh Garvey is an autistic author. She has a special interest in reading books, and writing books, which is why she became an author.

Before becoming an author, Niamh had a special interest in health and how the body worked, so she became a nurse. She worked as a nurse for a number of years and loved it. She also has a special interest in autism, so she studied for a Diploma in Autism Studies to learn everything she could about being autistic.

Niamh lives in Cork, Ireland, with her husband and three children. Oh, and four hens and two goldfish. She lives next to a big wood, where there is a rookery, and she pretends that the rooks are also her pets, but really the rooks pretend to be her friends so they can steal food from her vegetable garden.

About the illustrator

Rebecca (Bex) Burgess is a comic artist and illustrator working in the UK, creating award-winning published and small press work. Along with drawing comics for their day job, Rebecca also loves drawing webcomics in their free time. Being autistic, they are particularly passionate about bringing more autistic characters into stories! Outside of drawing and cuddling their cat, Rebecca also loves playing RPGs with friends, going on deep dives into history and growing vegetables in their humble Bristol garden.

The author's book for grown-ups

Looking After Your Autistic Self

A Personalised Self-Care Approach to
Managing Your Sensory and Emotional Well-Being

Niamh Garvey

Books we think you'll like

Page for doodling!

Page for doodling!

Page for doodling!

Page for doodling!

Page for doodling!

Page for doodling!

Page for doodling!

Page for doodling!